C000243213

QUEEN ELIZABETH II
REIGN IN PICTURES

"I declare before you all that my whole life whether it be long or short shall be devoted to your service and to the service of our great imperial family to which we all belong." This was Princess Elizabeth's promise to the British Commonwealth and Empire in a speech that was broadcast on the radio from Cape Town, South Africa, on 21 April 1947, her 21st birthday. The longest-serving monarch in British history, the Queen kept her promise to serve her people for 70 years.

As Britain and the Commonwealth mourn her passing, we pay tribute to Queen Elizabeth and her extraordinary reign. Her reign witnessed remarkable highs and lows, but she remained a steadfast and constant figure amid the social and political upheaval over the last seven decades. Join us as we look back at some of the key moments from her reign and personal life.

FUTURE

QUEEN
ELIZABETH II
REIGN IN PICTURES

Future PLC Quay House, The Ambury, Bath, BA1 1UA

Editorial
Editor **Jessica Leggett**
Senior Art Editor **Andy Downes**
Head of Art & Design **Greg Whitaker**
Editorial Director **Jon White**

Contributors
June Woolerton

Cover images
Getty Images

Photography
All copyrights and trademarks are recognised and respected

Advertising
Media packs are available on request
Commercial Director **Clare Dove**

International
Head of Print Licensing **Rachel Shaw**
licensing@futurenet.com
www.futurecontenthub.com

Circulation
Head of Newstrade **Tim Mathers**

Production
Head of Production **Mark Constance**
Production Project Manager **Matthew Eglinton**
Advertising Production Manager **Joanne Crosby**
Digital Editions Controller **Jason Hudson**
Production Managers **Keely Miller, Nola Cokely,
Vivienne Calvert, Fran Twentyman**

Printed i n the UK

Distributed by Marketforce, 5 Churchill Place, Canary Wharf, London, E14 5HU
www.marketforce.co.uk Tel: 0203 787 9001

Queen Elizabeth II: Reign in Pictures Second Edition (AHB5296)
© 2022 Future Publishing Limited

All content this edition of
Queen Elizabeth II: Reign in Pictures

We are committed to only using magazine paper which is derived from responsibly managed, certified forestry and chlorine-free manufacture. The paper in this bookazine was sourced and produced from sustainable managed forests, conforming to strict environmental and socioeconomic standards.

All contents © 2022 Future Publishing Limited or published under licence. All rights reserved. No part of this magazine may be used, stored, transmitted or reproduced in any way without the prior written permission of the publisher. Future Publishing Limited (company number 2008885) is registered in England and Wales. Registered office: Quay House, The Ambury, Bath BA1 1UA. All information contained in this publication is for information only and is, as far as we are aware, correct at the time of going to press. Future cannot accept any responsibility for errors or inaccuracies in such information. You are advised to contact manufacturers and retailers directly with regard to the price of products/services referred to in this publication. Apps and websites mentioned in this publication are not under our control. We are not responsible for their contents or any other changes or updates to them. This magazine is fully independent and not affiliated in any way with the companies mentioned herein.

Future plc is a public company quoted on the London Stock Exchange (symbol: FUTR)
www.futureplc.com

Chief executive **Zillah Byng-Thorne**
Non-executive chairman **Richard Huntingford**
Chief financial officer **Penny Ladkin-Brand**

Tel +44 (0)1225 442 244

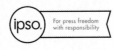

A New Era
6 February 1952

Princess Elizabeth and Prince Philip embarked on a tour of Australia and New Zealand, via Kenya, at the end of January 1952 on behalf of her father, King George VI, who was suffering from lung cancer and too ill to travel. The royal couple were in Kenya when the king died in his sleep at Sandringham on 6 February. Philip was the one who broke the news to Elizabeth about her father's death, and the couple immediately returned to London, where they were greeted by Prime Minister Winston Churchill. Elizabeth was a princess when she left Britain, but she returned as a queen.

THE CORONATION CEREMONY
2 June 1953

Queen Elizabeth's coronation took place in Westminster Abbey, over a year after her accession, to allow for her father's mourning. Elizabeth was the 39th monarch to be crowned at Westminster Abbey, with over 8,000 people in attendance. She wore a coronation gown designed by Norman Hartnell, embroidered with emblems of the United Kingdom and Commonwealth. Her husband, the Duke of Edinburgh, is shown here paying homage to his queen and wife. The ceremony was televised on the BBC, which Philip had encouraged as Chair of the Coronation Commission, and it was watched by 27 million people in the UK and millions more around the world.

© Getty

CELEBRATING WITH HER PEOPLE
2 June 1953

After the coronation ceremony, the Queen returned to Buckingham Palace in the Gold State Coach - a journey that she revealed in 2018 was "horrible" and "not very comfortable". She appeared on the balcony with her family to wave to the crowd, wearing the Imperial State Crown and Royal Robes. In this photo, the Queen is seen with Prince Philip, Prince Charles and Princess Anne. That day, she appeared on the balcony several times, including to watch a flypast over Buckingham Palace and to turn on the 'lights of London', which included cascading lights down The Mall and floodlights at the National Gallery and the Tower of London.

"SHE APPEARED ON THE BALCONY WITH HER FAMILY TO WAVE TO THE CROWD, WEARING THE IMPERIAL STATE CROWN AND ROYAL ROBES"

© Getty

"THOUSANDS OF PEOPLE
LINED THE RIVER THAMES
AT THE END OF THE
TOUR TO SEE THE QUEEN
RETURN ON THE ROYAL
YACHT BRITANNIA"

CORONATION TOUR OF THE COMMONWEALTH
November 1953 – May 1954

After her coronation, the Queen embarked on her longest ever Commonwealth tour. She was accompanied by Prince Philip, Prince Charles and Princess Anne, with the family visiting 13 countries across Africa, Asia, Australasia and the West Indies. The Queen is seen here with Prince Philip at a Māori reception at Arawa Park Racecourse in Rotorua, New Zealand, wearing a Korowai Māori kiwi feather cloak that was given to her as a gift. Thousands of people lined the River Thames at the end of the tour to see the Queen return on the Royal Yacht Britannia. She was the most well-travelled monarch in British history.

© Getty

A FINE FAREWELL
4 April 1955

On the eve of his retirement, Prime Minister Winston Churchill hosted a dinner at 10 Downing Street, attended by Queen Elizabeth and the Duke of Edinburgh. Churchill and the Queen had developed a close relationship, with the former being a close friend of her late father, as well as helping to guide the young monarch through the first three years of her reign. It was a great honour for Churchill to host the Queen and although he declined her offer to make him Duke of London, he did accept the Order of the Garter.

© Getty

15

FIRST TELEVISED CHRISTMAS SPEECH

25 December 1957

The Queen made history when she gave her first televised Christmas Speech from the Long Library at Sandringham in 1957. The monarch's Christmas Day speech is a tradition that dates back to Elizabeth's grandfather, King George V, who delivered the first one over the radio in 1932. In her speech, which was broadcast live, the Queen noted: "25 years ago, my grandfather broadcast the first of these Christmas messages. Today is another landmark because television has made it possible for many of you to see me in your homes on Christmas Day." She is smiling at Prince Philip in this photograph.

© Getty

© Getty

BIRTH OF PRINCES ANDREW & EDWARD

19 February 1960 & 10 March 1964

In 1960, ten years after her second child and only daughter, Princess Anne, the Queen gave birth to Prince Andrew, the first child born to the reigning monarch in 103 years. When the Queen gave birth to Edward in 1964, it is said that Prince Philip was present in the delivery room after she read that fathers should be present during childbirth. Philip was the first royal father in modern history to witness the birth of one of his children. The Queen, holding Prince Edward, and Philip are photographed here on the balcony of Buckingham Palace during the Trooping of the Colour in June 1964.

MEETING THE KENNEDYS
15 June 1961

Just a few months after taking office, President John F Kennedy and his wife, Jackie, visited Buckingham Palace, where the Queen held a banquet in their honour. JFK was assassinated just two years later in November 1963, and Prince Philip attended the funeral alone as Elizabeth was pregnant with Prince Edward. However, she did open a memorial for Kennedy at Runnymede, Berkshire, in 1965. During her seven decades on the throne, the Queen met 13 out of the 14 US presidents that held the office during her reign; the only one she never met was Kennedy's successor, Lyndon B Johnson.

©Getty

AN ICONIC MOMENT

20 November 1961

Ghana gained independence from the United Kingdom in 1957, and the monarchy was abolished in 1960, leaving Ghana as a Commonwealth republic. Despite concerns about Ghana's ties to the Soviet Union, the Queen insisted on visiting the country in 1961 because she wanted it to remain in the Commonwealth. It was her first visit to Ghana and at a farewell ball held at State House in Accra, the Queen famously danced with Ghanaian president Kwame Nkrumah. In this photo, they're dancing to a special version of 'High Life' called 'Welcome Your Majesty' that was composed for the occasion.

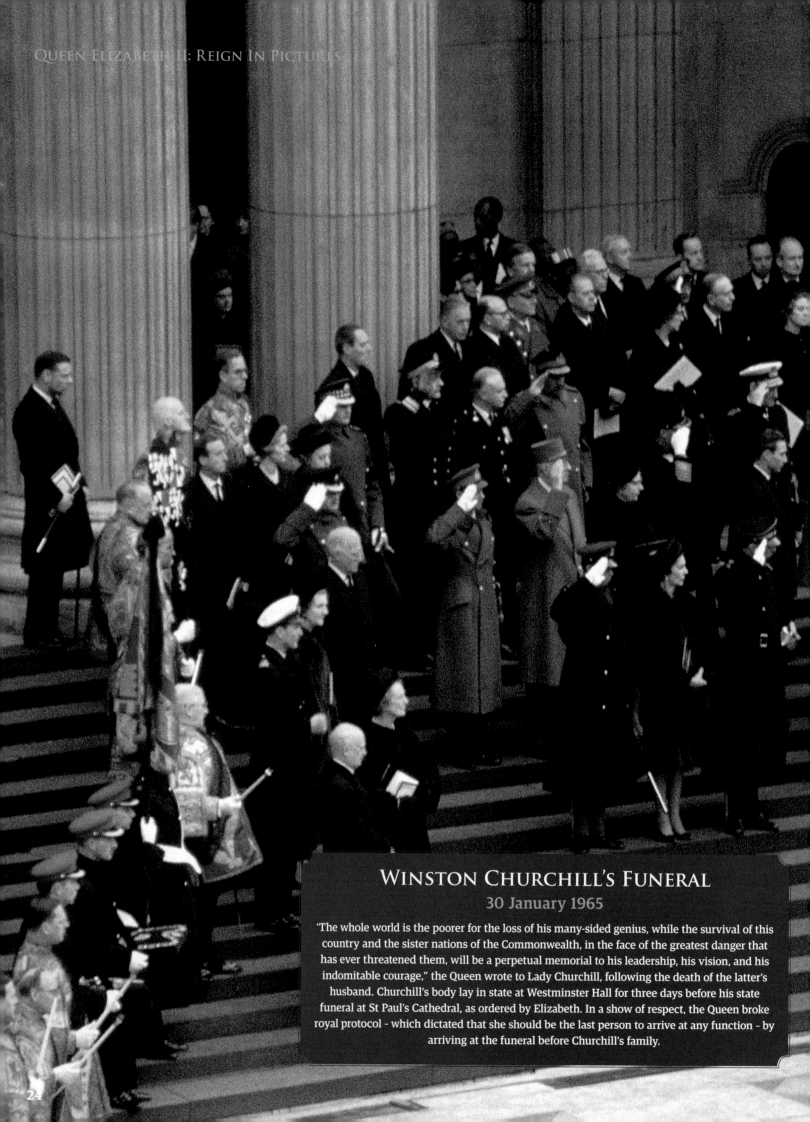

WINSTON CHURCHILL'S FUNERAL
30 January 1965

'The whole world is the poorer for the loss of his many-sided genius, while the survival of this country and the sister nations of the Commonwealth, in the face of the greatest danger that has ever threatened them, will be a perpetual memorial to his leadership, his vision, and his indomitable courage," the Queen wrote to Lady Churchill, following the death of the latter's husband. Churchill's body lay in state at Westminster Hall for three days before his state funeral at St Paul's Cathedral, as ordered by Elizabeth. In a show of respect, the Queen broke royal protocol - which dictated that she should be the last person to arrive at any function - by arriving at the funeral before Churchill's family.

STATE VISIT TO WEST GERMANY
27 May 1965

The Queen's historic visit to Berlin, West Germany, was the culmination of a 20-year reconciliation process following the end of World War II. 'Queen fever' quickly hit the capital, with over a million people lining the streets to cheer on the Queen and Prince Philip as they left Charlottenburg Schloss in an open-topped car, after attending a reception in their honour. The Queen also delivered a speech in which she pledged her support to those in West Berlin and at the end of her visit, she signed the city's Golden Book at Schöneberg Town Hall.

© Getty

A HISTORIC VICTORY
30 July 1966

After watching England defeat West Germany 4-2 in extra time in the 1966 World Cup final at Wembley Stadium, the Queen presented the Jules Rimet trophy to England captain Bobby Moore. A total of 93,000 people were in the stadium to witness one of the most historic sporting events in British history. The Queen recalled the moment 55 years later, when she wrote to England manager Gareth Southgate and the England team, praising them for their "spirit, commitment, and pride" after they reached the Euro 2020 final.

© Getty

THE ABERFAN DISASTER
21 October 1966

Tragedy struck when a coal tip in Aberfan, Wales, collapsed on a local school and killed 144 people, including 116 children. The Queen arrived eight days after the devastating landslide, paying a visit to comfort the families of people who lost their lives in the avalanche. She was greatly affected by the catastrophe and apparently regretted her delay in arriving at Aberfan, a decision she made believing that her presence would distract rescue and recovery efforts. This moment was one of the few times in her reign that the Queen cried in public and she later returned to Aberfan on several occasions.

© Getty

A Glimpse of Royal Life
21 June 1969

Royal Family was a television documentary that aired on BBC 1 and ITV, documenting the day-to-day life of the Queen and her family. It was the idea of William Heseltine, the royal Press Secretary, and John Brabourne, a television producer, in an attempt to show that the royal family were not out of touch. Over 30 million people in the United Kingdom tuned in, and an estimated 350 million people watched it around the world. The documentary, which aired for the last time in 1977, was criticised for revealing too much about the monarchy, and the Queen banned it from

THE QUEEN PRESENTS HER HEIR TO WALES

1 July 1969

The Queen created her eldest son Prince of Wales in 1958, but it was another 11 years before his investiture in a ceremony designed as much for TV as it was for history. Millions watched the spectacle at Caernarfon Castle where Charles was presented with the rod, sceptre, coronet, ring and mantle of his role, and pledged to be his mother's "liege man of life and limb". Welsh nationalists staged protests before the ceremony and two were killed just before the investiture when their homemade bomb detonated. Charles, who had spent time learning Welsh, then spent a week touring his new principality.

© Getty

THE QUEEN'S FAITHFUL COMPANIONS

4 February 1970

There is perhaps no image of Queen Elizabeth more iconic than that of her accompanied by her beloved corgis. The Queen had owned Pembroke Welsh Corgis since she was a child, with her father bringing home her first, Dookie, in 1933. For her 18th birthday, the Queen was given a corgi named Susan, who famously accompanied Elizabeth and the Duke of Edinburgh on their honeymoon in 1947. The Queen owned over 30 corgis during her long reign, many of whom were descended from Susan, and she also owned cocker spaniels as well as dorgis, a dachshund-corgi crossbreed.

THE WINDSOR WALKABOUTS BEGIN
1 May 1970

Walkabouts are a staple of modern royal life, but they were only introduced on a tour of Australia in 1970 and proved instantly popular. Elizabeth ditched the usual approach of waving at crowds from a distance and instead strolled over to talk to them directly. The idea had come from her private secretary, Australian Sir William Heseltine, whose attempts to make the royals more accessible also included allowing cameras behind palace doors for a TV documentary. Charles, Philip and Anne were also on the tour, and her husband and daughter would be criticised for appearing to swear during their first attempts at walkabouts.

© Getty

A Beloved Hideaway
1 October 1972

Balmoral, the Queen's country estate in the Scottish Highlands, has been a holiday home for the royal family since the reign of Queen Victoria. The Queen spent every summer at Balmoral, where the family enjoyed a range of country pursuits and relaxed away from the press, and it was often said to be her favourite residence. It was at Balmoral that Prince Philip proposed to Elizabeth, and they even spent part of their honeymoon at Birkhall, a country home on the estate. The Queen and Prince Philip can be seen here walking together among the Highland cattle in the grounds of Balmoral.

BORROWED DIAMONDS AT A CONTROVERSIAL CONCERT

3 January 1973

Britain's entry into the EEC (later the EU) in January 1973 was marked by an 11-day festival of events that started with the Queen attending a gala concert at Covent Garden, accompanied by the then-prime minister, Edward Heath. The musical evening included a special *Fanfare for Europe* by composer Edward Gregson. Government funding for the festival, which also included a star-studded football match at Wembley, proved controversial, and jeers were heard before the concert. The Queen also had to borrow a tiara for the event at the last minute as her own broke in the car on the way to Covent Garden.

© Getty

"THE SUMMER SAW THE TOUR TAKE IN ALL FOUR NATIONS OF THE UK WITH VISITS TO 36 COUNTIES"

A Record-Breaking Tour for the Silver Jubilee

2 February 1977

For the first major jubilee of her reign, her silver celebration, the Queen completed the most extensive tour ever undertaken by a British monarch. In early 1977, she headed to Samoa, Tonga and Fiji before her Commonwealth trips took her to New Zealand, Australia and India. The summer saw the tour take in all four nations of the UK with visits to 36 counties throughout June, July and August. In the last part of her Silver Jubilee year, the Queen visited Canada, the British Virgin Islands, the Bahamas and Barbados with big crowds turning out at every stop.

Getty

HISTORIC STATE VISIT BREAKS DOWN RELIGIOUS BARRIERS
17 October 1980

The Queen became the first British monarch to make a state visit to the Vatican after accepting an invitation from Pope John Paul II. Although she had been received by previous popes at the Vatican, the state visit was seen as the development of closer bonds between the Church of England and the Catholic Church. Wearing the traditional black gown and veil, the Queen delivered a speech asking the pope to come to the UK on a pastoral trip. When John Paul II arrived in England two years later, the first reigning pope to visit the country, Elizabeth hosted him at Buckingham Palace.

© Getty

"THE STUFF OF WHICH FAIRYTALES ARE MADE"

29 July 1981

The wedding of Prince Charles and Lady Diana Spencer was a moment of personal happiness for the Queen, but also a promise of dynastic continuity. Their romance had captured imaginations to such an extent that at their marriage, at St Paul's Cathedral, the Archbishop of Canterbury told the 3,500 guests it was the "stuff of which fairytales are made". A TV audience of 750 million around the world celebrated, while huge crowds cheered as the newlyweds kissed on the balcony of Buckingham Palace in a romantic gesture that set the seal on the "wedding of the century".

© Getty

BEHIND THE CAMERA
16 May 1982

The Queen was one of the world's most photographed women, but she actually enjoyed being behind the camera. Queen Elizabeth had been an avid photographer since she was a child and she shared the hobby with her beloved father. She was captured numerous times throughout her reign snapping pictures of her own, and she was even filmed taking photographs as she returned from her Commonwealth tour in 1954. It is said that the Queen frequently took photos when her family was gathered together and that she always travelled with her photo albums.

"SHE WAS GIVEN HER FIRST HORSE, A SHETLAND PONY, WHEN SHE WAS JUST FOUR YEARS OLD"

AN EQUESTRIAN AT HEART
8 June 1982

The Queen had loved horse riding since she was a young girl. She was given her first horse, a Shetland pony, when she was just four years old, and the Queen was seen still riding her horses in 2021, at the age of 95. It was a passion that she had shared with her daughter, Princess Anne, and Anne's daughter, Zara Tindall, who have both competed in equestrian events at the Olympics. The Queen was photographed on horseback several times throughout her reign - here she is pictured riding in Windsor Great Park with President Ronal Reagan during his state visit to the UK in 1982.

A Grandmother Again, to a Future King

21 June 1982

In the fading light of Midsummer's Night, it was announced that the Princess of Wales had given birth to a son and so secured the direct line of succession to the Queen's throne. Within hours, the Prince of Wales emerged from St Mary's Hospital, London, to huge cheers and headed into the crowds for a walkabout. Thousands gathered at Buckingham Palace to see the official statement confirming the arrival of a future king. The new baby had his first photocall the next day when he was taken home. He was christened William Arthur Philip Louis in August at Buckingham Palace.

© Getty

TROOPING THE COLOUR
11 June 1983

Trooping the Colour is a ceremony performed by the regiments of the British Army in celebration of the sovereign's official birthday. It has been performed for over 270 years and the Queen attended the event every single year during her reign apart from 1955, when it was cancelled due to a national rail strike. In 1981, both the Queen and her horse were startled when Marcus Sarjeant fired six blank rounds at her as she rode down The Mall, but she remained unharmed. The Queen is pictured here riding side-saddled at the 1983 ceremony with Prince Philip and Prince Charles behind her, and from 1987 onwards, she rode in a carriage.

© Getty

"HUNDREDS OF PEOPLE FORMED
A HUMAN CHAIN TO REMOVE
PRICELESS ROYAL ARTEFACTS FROM
THE PATH OF THE FIRE"

THE DISASTER THAT SET FIRE TO AN "ANNUS HORRIBILIS"
20 November 1992

A fire broke out at Windsor Castle when a curtain brushed against a faulty spotlight in the Private Chapel. Within hours, over 225 firefighters and 39 engines were tackling the flames while hundreds of people formed a human chain to remove priceless royal artefacts from the path of the fire. The blaze burned for 15 hours and left the State Apartments, including St George's Hall, badly damaged. Prince Philip oversaw restoration work but the debate over costs led to Buckingham Palace being opened to tourists and the Queen paying income tax. Days after the fire, Elizabeth described 1992 as her

"THIS WONDERFUL MAN" AND "MY FRIEND, ELIZABETH"

20 March 1995

The Queen made a state visit to South Africa just months after Nelson Mandela had been elected the country's president in the nation's first full and free polls. She arrived in Cape Town on 19 March for a six-day trip, which also took her to Port Elizabeth, Durban, Pretoria and Johannesburg, and presented Nelson Mandela with the Order of Merit. She maintained a strong relationship with Nelson Mandela, who called her "my dear friend Elizabeth", and happily agreed to his request to abandon the traditional banquet on his state visit to Britain, instead enjoying a concert with him at the Royal Albert Hall.

© Getty

61

THE MONARCHY ROCKED BY THE DEATH OF A PRINCESS
31 August 1997

The Queen faced one of the greatest crises of her reign when her former daughter-in-law, Diana, died following a car crash in Paris alongside her new partner, Dodi Fayed. The shock of Diana's death was followed by widespread mourning, but the Queen's decision to remain at Balmoral, to care for William and Harry, led to huge criticisms and papers demanding "show us you care". There were concerns the Queen would be heckled when she visited some of the floral tributes left for Diana. However, her clear support for her grandsons, and a televised address paying tribute to the princess on the eve of her funeral, saw public anger fade.

THE COUNCIL ESTATE QUEEN
7 July 1999

During a visit to Glasgow, the Queen popped in for tea at the council estate home of Susan McCarron. For 15 minutes, the two women chatted while Mrs McCarron's ten-year-old son, James, sat on the sofa with a lady-in-waiting, somewhat bemused. Just two years after the death of Diana, Princess of Wales, visits like this were designed to make the Queen more accessible. Susan McCarron was full of praise for her royal visitor, who enjoyed the tea but didn't touch the biscuits. "I found her very easy to talk to," she said as the Queen departed.

Getty

THE END OF AN ERA
9 February & 30 March 2002

On 9 February 2002, the Queen's only sister, Princess Margaret, died after a long illness. Days later, the Queen Mother was helicoptered to Windsor for the funeral of her younger child. Her own health was failing and on 30 March 2002, she died at the age of 101 with the Queen holding her hand. Over 200,000 people filed past her coffin as it lay in state at Westminster Hall with the final guard made up of her four grandsons. Her state funeral, on 9 April 2002, was followed by burial at St George's Chapel, Windsor, alongside her husband, King George VI, and the ashes of Princess Margaret.

© Getty

A VERY MODERN JUBILEE
4 June 2002

As the Golden Jubilee celebrations came to an end, the Queen rode down The Mall in the Golden Coronation Coach to the cheers of huge crowds on her way to a service of thanksgiving at St Paul's Cathedral. The 50th anniversary of her reign had been marked with tradition including street parties and chains of beacons across the UK. However, it was the "people's" concerts at Buckingham Palace that set the tone for the celebrations, with Queen guitarist, Brian May, playing the National Anthem from the roof. Early fears the Golden Jubilee might be a flop were proved wrong.

A SEAL OF APPROVAL FOR A CONTROVERSIAL ROYAL ROMANCE
9 April 2005

The Queen wasn't present when her eldest son married his long-term partner, Camilla Parker Bowles, in a civil ceremony at Windsor Guildhall, but she was in the congregation as the couple's marriage was blessed the same day in a service at St George's Chapel. Ahead of the wedding, it was announced that Camilla would be known as the Duchess of Cornwall rather than Princess of Wales as her relationship with Charles during the later years of his marriage to Diana continued to cause controversy. The wedding was held on Grand National Day with the Queen remarking at the reception: "The couple have finally arrived in the winner's enclosure."

A ROMANTIC MOMENT FOR A HISTORY-MAKING COUPLE

20 November 2007

To mark 60 years of marriage, the Queen and the Duke of Edinburgh recreated a photograph taken of them walking at Broadlands soon after their 1947 wedding. The rather personal moment was in contrast to the major celebrations held for their diamond wedding anniversary, which saw thousands take part in a thanksgiving service at Westminster Abbey. The Prince of Wales and the Duchess of Cornwall hosted a special dinner at Clarence House, which finished with more historic photos, including one of the couple with the royal family. The Queen and Prince Philip were the first British monarch and consort to mark 60 years of marriage.

© Getty

BREAKING PROTOCOL WITH A NEW FRIEND

1 April 2009

al protocol dictates that no one
es the Queen, but in 2009, then-
st lady Michelle Obama appeared
a hug from the monarch. At the
a long reception at Buckingham
Mrs Obama put her arm around
een, who returned the gesture,
ng the briefest of high-power
A huge debate broke out about
r royal rules had been broken,
elle Obama later said she wasn't
the protocol while her husband
that the Queen hadn't minded.
mas returned to Buckingham
2011 for a state visit, but there
re no more royal hugs.

© Getty

THE WEDDING OF A FUTURE KING AND QUEEN
29 April 2011

Almost a decade after they met, Prince William and Catherine Middleton married at Westminster Abbey before a congregation that mingled European royalty with stars including the Beckhams. The bride, in bespoke Alexander McQueen gown, wore a tiara loaned to her by the Queen and carried a posy that included 'Sweet William' flowers. The groom was given the Dukedom of Cambridge by his grandmother on the day of his wedding. Hundreds of thousands gathered to cheer the couple on the Buckingham Palace balcony. There were over 5,000 street parties in the UK, while two billion people are reported to have watched the wedding on TV.

© Getty

A HISTORIC STATE VISIT TO IRELAND
17–20 May 2011

The Queen arrived in Dublin dressed in green for the first state visit by a British monarch to the Republic of Ireland. Seen as symbolic of improving relations between the two countries following decades of violent dispute, it drew some criticism from Irish republicans and involved the country's biggest-ever security operation. She was welcomed by President Mary McAleese, who was overwhelmed when the Queen began her state banquet speech in Gaelic. The visit took in the National War Memorial Gardens and Croke Park, where sports fans had been killed by British forces in 1920. The Queen carried out a walkabout in Cork as the visit ended.

© Getty

THE DIAMOND QUEEN LIGHTS UP LONDON
4 June 2012

The Queen was guest of honour at a Buckingham Palace concert held as her Diamond Jubilee drew to a close. Over 12,000 people won free tickets for the event, while around 250,000 more gathered in The Mall to watch on giant screens as stars including Sir Paul McCartney and Kylie Minogue took to a stage built around the Victoria Memorial. Dame Shirley Bassey sang 'Diamonds are Forever', while concert organiser, Gary Barlow, led a performance of the jubilee anthem, 'Sing'. Prince Philip was taken ill hours beforehand and had to miss the show, which ended with the Queen lighting the traditional jubilee beacon.

© Getty

AN OLYMPIC SURPRISE
FROM THE QUEEN
27 July 2012

The Queen surprised the world as all eyes fell on London for the 2012 Summer Olympics. As the Opening Ceremony got underway, Danny Boyle's spectacular show went inside Buckingham Palace where Daniel Craig's James Bond found himself playing opposite the Queen. With the help of a corgi and a straight-faced footman, the duo marched out of the palace and into history as the film then mocked up Elizabeth II parachuting into the opening ceremony before the Queen walked out to formally inaugurate the Games, which went on to be one of the most successful ever.

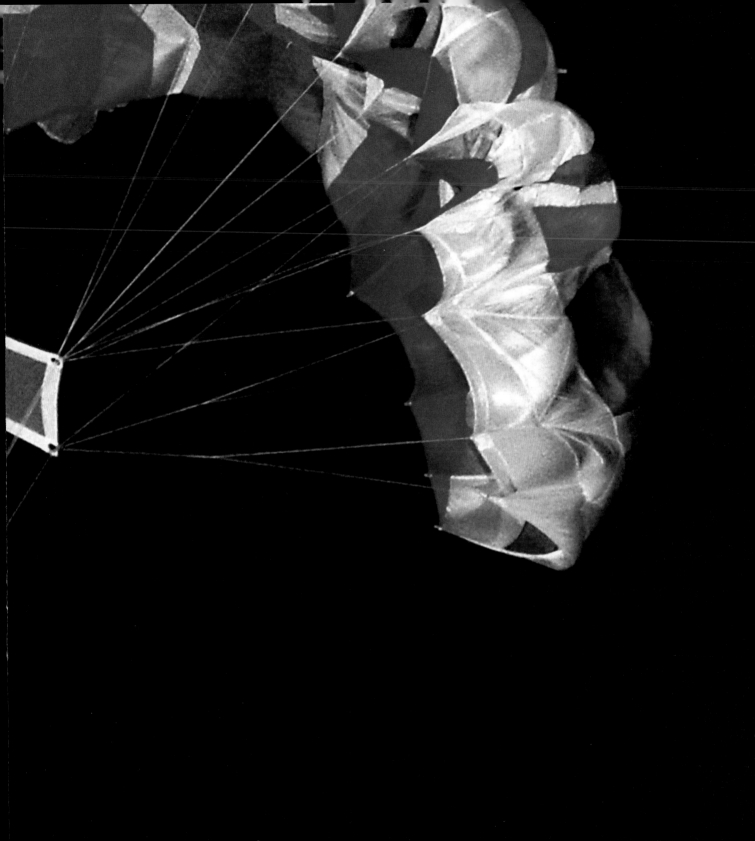

"THE FILM THEN MOCKED UP
ELIZABETH II PARACHUTING INTO
THE OPENING CEREMONY"

© Getty

ALL THE QUEEN'S HORSES
20 June 2013

The Queen was a huge horseracing fan, and she was frequently seen getting animated while watching a race. She owned and bred thoroughbred horses for racing, and she was named the British flat racing Champion Owner in 1954 and 1957. With the exception of the Derby, she had bred and owned the winner of every British Classic, and she was inducted into the Qipco British Champions Series Hall of Fame in 2021 for her contribution to British flat racing. The Queen is seen here with her bloodstock and racing advisor, John Warren, cheering on her horse, Estimate, to win the Gold Cup on Ladies' Day at Ascot Racecourse in 2013 - the first time the cup

© Getty

THE QUEEN AND THREE KINGS IN WAITING
22 July 2013

The birth of George Alexander Louis, Prince William and Catherine's eldest child, meant that for the first time in over a century, a British monarch had three direct heirs in the line of succession. The Queen and the future kings posed for a historic 'four generations' photo at Prince George's christening. Ahead of the prince's birth, the Queen had changed the succession rules to ensure that had a princess been born first, she would have retained her rights over a younger brother. George, third in line to the throne, had been seen many times with his 'Gan-Gan', who was reported to be a doting great-grandmother.

THE QUEEN, THE LORDS AND THE COMMONS

27 May 2015

The State Opening of Parliament was one of the most important events in the Queen's year and she only missed it twice during her long reign. Steeped in tradition and ceremony, it marks the official opening of the parliamentary year and it is the only time all three parts of the legislature - the Crown, the Lords and the Commons - are together. The Queen's Speech set out the government's plans and it was written for her to deliver. The Queen stopped wearing the Imperial State Crown for the ceremony in 2019 because of its weight; instead it sat on a table beside her.

© Getty

IT IS ALL FUN AND GAMES
5 September 2015

The Queen regularly attended the Braemar Gathering, the most famous Highland games competition in the world, during her annual summer holiday to Scotland. It is held close to the Balmoral estate and it has been a tradition for the royal family to attend the games for over 170 years, ever since Queen Victoria attended the Braemar Gathering in 1848. The Queen was the patron for the event and the 'Chieftan', where competitions such as hammer tossing, a tug of war and Highland dancing are held. She was often seen having a whale of a time with a blanket on her lap and surrounded by her family.

The Queen was reluctant to mark the moment she overtook her great-great-grandmother, Victoria, as Britain's longest-reigning monarch, but celebrations were widespread. A flotilla of ships processed along the Thames while the House of Commons paused its daily business so MPs could pay tribute to Elizabeth. The Queen travelled by train to Scotland where people gathered along railway banks to catch a glimpse of the record-breaking ruler. Her response was understated, as she thanked crowds for their kindness, adding: "Inevitably a long life can pass by many milestones – my own is no exception."

"THE HOUSE OF COMMONS PAUSED ITS DAILY BUSINESS SO MPS COULD PAY TRIBUTE TO ELIZABETH"

© Getty

THE QUEEN'S GREEN PLANET HITS TV SCREENS

16 April 2018

The Queen allowed the TV cameras into Buckingham Palace for a special programme with Sir David Attenborough to highlight a royal environmental project. *The Queen's Green Planet* focused on the Commonwealth Canopy, a network of protected forest projects being established around the world. The Queen, who had persuaded many leaders to take part herself, aimed for it to spread across every Commonwealth nation. She explained its significance and the chance it could change the climate for the better. There was time for humour, too. As a helicopter interrupted their chat, the Queen remarked: "Sounds like President Trump - or Obama."

© Shutterstock

A VERY MODERN ROYAL WEDDING
19 May 2018

Meghan Markle became the first person of African-American descent to marry into the royal family when she wed Prince Harry at St George's Chapel, Windsor. The ceremony at the ancient chapel reflected her modern celebrity with stars including George Clooney and Oprah Winfrey attending. The groom handpicked flowers from the couple's garden for the wedding bouquet, while guests, including the Queen, lunched on bowl food and sponge cake at a very 21st-century reception in St George's Hall. Hundreds of thousands turned out to cheer the new Duke and Duchess of Sussex, but two years later, they stepped back from public life.

© Getty

THE QUEEN'S PATRONAGES

6 November 2019

Queen Elizabeth was the patron of more than 600 charities and organisations, such as the British Red Cross and Cancer Research UK, located in the United Kingdom and throughout the Commonwealth. During her reign, she raised billions for charity and brought publicity for many of them. She supported a diverse range of charities, social clubs, armed services, art organisations, schools and universities, as well as a variety of issues including wildlife preservation and the environment. Many of them reflected her personal interests too; for example, she was the patron of the National Horseracing Museum and the Jockey Club.

A UNIQUE INVESTITURE FOR A NATIONAL HERO

17 July 2020

Captain Sir Thomas Moore's attempts to walk 100 laps of his garden before his 100th birthday to raise money for the NHS had inspired millions during the first lockdown. His efforts brought in over £32 million and he was given a special nomination for a knighthood by Prime Minister Boris Johnson. His investiture took place on the Quadrangle at Windsor Castle. The Queen used a sword that had belonged to her father, King George VI, to knight Captain Sir Tom as his family watched on in the first-ever socially distanced investiture.

© Getty

THE FINAL FAREWELL TO HER 'STRENGTH AND STAY'

9 April 2021

"It is with deep sorrow that Her Majesty The Queen announces the death of her beloved husband." This simple statement, released just hours after Prince Philip's passing, confirmed the ending of a partnership that had endured for three-quarters of a century. The couple had spent the last weeks of Philip's life together, at Windsor Castle, after the prince's stay in hospital earlier in 2021. Covid restrictions meant just 30 people attended Prince Philip's funeral at St George's Chapel. The Duke's coffin was carried on a special Land Rover he designed himself. The Queen observed all pandemic rules and mourned her husband alone.

A DRIVING FORCE
2 July 2021

The Queen had always held a love for driving. During World War II, a 19-year-old Princess Elizabeth joined the Auxiliary Territorial Service and trained as a driver and mechanic. In 2003, the Queen famously took Abdullah, Crown Prince of Saudi Arabia, for a drive in her Land Rover while he was visiting her at Balmoral in Scotland. This reportedly left the Crown Prince terrified as he was unaware that she would be driving him, and it is often hailed as a feminist move by the Queen, as women in Saudi Arabia were banned from driving at the time. Queen Elizabeth had stopped driving on public roads in 2019, but she was pictured here behind the wheel at the Royal Windsor Horse Show in 2021.

© Getty

Emotion and Grief in her Most Personal Christmas Speech

25 December 2021

The Queen's Christmas Day Speech in 2021 was the most personal she had ever given as she paid tribute to "my beloved Philip". Sitting by a photo of them on their diamond wedding anniversary and wearing the brooch she had chosen for their honeymoon photocall, she spoke movingly of his life and legacy as well as his loss, revealing "that mischievous, inquiring twinkle at the end was as bright as when I first saw him". The Queen also looked ahead to her Platinum Jubilee, which she described as a chance for people to "enjoy a sense of togetherness".

© Getty

A HISTORIC JUBILEE
2-5 June 2022

On 6 February, the Queen became the first British monarch to reach her Platinum Jubilee. Events were held across Britain and the Commonwealth to celebrate her 70 years on the throne throughout the year, ending with a four-day bank holiday in June in the UK. The Queen showed her sense of humour by participating in a pre-recorded sketch with Paddington Bear for the BBC's 'Platinum Party at the Palace', which was one of many celebrations held in London. The Queen twice appeared with her family on the balcony of Buckingham Palace, thrilling the crowds who had come to celebrate her extraordinary reign.

© Getty

DEDICATED TO DUTY
6 September 2022

As her health deteriorated in the last few years of her reign, Queen Elizabeth undertook fewer public engagements, with Prince Charles and other members of the royal family taking on more responsibilities. But she never lost sight of her sense of obligation, and she remained devoted to carrying out her constitutional duties as monarch. She accepted Boris Johnson's resignation at Balmoral Castle as one of her last official acts as monarch, and she immediately appointed Liz Truss to take his place as prime minister. Since they typically took place at Buckingham Palace, these meetings were unusual. However, it was decided that the Queen should stay at Balmoral Castle, where she was enjoying her annual summer vacation, since it was more convenient for her to do so.

© Getty

SAYING GOODBYE TO A BELOVED QUEEN
19 September 2022

With her two eldest children by her side, Queen Elizabeth passed away at Balmoral Castle on 8 September, just two days after appointing Liz Truss as the new prime minister of the United Kingdom. Her body lay in state at Westminster Hall with members of the public queuing for hours to file past her coffin. A state funeral for the Queen was held on 19 September at Westminster Abbey, and dignitaries from all over the world were present. Her coffin was then transported to Windsor for a committal service at St George's Chapel. She was interred in a private ceremony that evening in the King George VI Memorial Chapel, laid to rest with her husband, Prince Philip, her parents and her sister.

© Getty

★ ON SALE NOW! ★

A tribute to the life and reign of Queen Elizabeth II

We explore the woman who has ruled over generations of her subjects. From her worst year – or 'annus horribilis' – to her triumphs, we remember a queen who devoted herself to her country and the people within it.

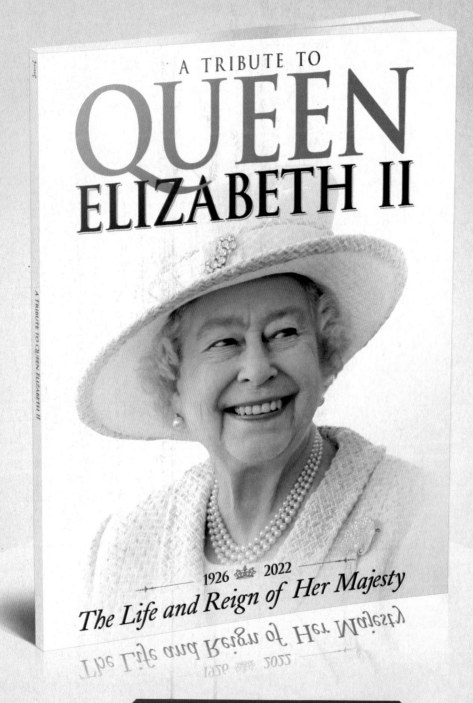

Ordering is easy. Go online at:

WWW.MAGAZINESDIRECT.COM

Or get it from selected supermarkets & newsagents

FUTURE